Nails

Written by Paul Jennings

Illustrated by Jill Carter Hansen

Lehman's father sat still on his cane chair. Too still.

A hot breeze ruffled his hair. He stared out of the window at the island. But he did not see. He did not move. He did not know that Lehman was alone.

But the boy knew. He realized he was trapped. Their boat had sunk in the storm. And their radio had gone with it. There was not another soul for a thousand miles. Lehman was rich. The house was his now. The whole island belonged to him. The golden beach. The high hill. The palms. And the little pier where their boat had once bobbed and rocked.

He had no more tears. He had cried them all. Every one. He wanted to rush over and hug his father back to life. He wanted to see that twisted grin again. "Dad, Dad," he called.

But the dead man had no reply for his son.

Lehman knew that he had to do something. He had to close his father's eyes. That was the first thing. But he couldn't bring himself to do it. What if they wouldn't move? What if they were brittle? Or cold? Or soggy?

And then what? He couldn't leave his father there. Sitting stiff and silent in the terrible heat. He had to bury him. Where? How? He knew that no one would come. The blue sea was endless. Unbroken. Unfriendly to a boy on his own.

Lehman started to scratch nervously. His nails were growing. More of them all the time.

He decided to do nothing for a bit longer. He sat and sat and sat. And remembered how it was when they had come to the island. Just the two of them.

4

"Is that where we live?" said Lehman.

They both looked at the tumbledown hut on top of the hill. "We'll fix it up in no time," said Dad. "It'll soon be like it was in the old days. When I first came here. As good as new."

And after a while it was. It was home. Lehman became used to it. Even though he was lonely. Every morning he did his schoolwork. Dad told him which books to read. And how to do his math. Then he left Lehman alone with his studies. And disappeared along the beach.

Dad searched the shore. But he never let Lehman go with him. He took his camera and his knapsack. And his shovel. He peered out into the endless sea. He dug in the golden sand. And every lunch time he returned with rocks and strange objects from the sea.

5

"One day I'll hit the jackpot," he said for the thousandth time. "Maybe tomorrow. Tomorrow I'll find one. Tomorrow will be the day. You'll see." Then he grew sad. "There were plenty here once." He dumped his sack in the corner. It thumped heavily on the floor.

"Let's see what you've got," said Lehman.

Dad shook his head. "When I find what I'm looking for, you'll be the first to know." He picked up the sack and took it into his room. He shut the door with a smile.

Lehman knew what his father was doing. He was putting his finds into the old box. The sea chest with the heavy brass lock. Lehman longed to take a look. He wanted to know what his father was searching for. But it was a secret.

He began to scratch his fingers. Just as Dad came out of his room. "I've told you not to do that," said Dad.

"I'm itchy," said Lehman. "On the fingers. And the toes."

"Eczema," Dad told him. "I used to get it when I was a boy. It'll go when the wind changes." But he didn't look too sure. He examined the red lumps growing behind Lehman's fingernails. Then he stamped out of the hut.

Lehman stared around the silent bungalow. He was lonely. Dad was good company. But he was a man. Lehman wanted friends. And his mother. He picked up her photograph. A lovely, sad face. Staring at him from the oval frame. "Where did you go?" whispered Lehman. "I can't even remember you."

The face seemed to say that it knew. Understood. But it was only a photo of a woman's head. A woman lost in the past. In her hair she wore a golden clip set with pearls.

During the day, Lehman kept the photo on the kitchen table where he worked. And at night he placed it on his bedside table. It watched over him while he slept.

Lehman sighed and closed his book. He looked up as Dad came back carrying some potatoes from their vegetable patch. "I'm going early in the morning," he said. "Just go on with the work I set for you today. I'll be back at lunch time."

"Let me come with you," pleaded Lehman.

His father looked at him in silence. Then he said, "When I find what I'm looking for, then I'll take you."

"It's not fair," shouted Lehman. "I'm all alone here. Every morning. You owe it to me to tell me what you're looking for. I don't even know what we're doing here."

"I can't tell you," said Dad slowly. "Not yet. Trust me."

That night, in bed, Lehman's eczema was worse. He scratched his itching fingers and toes until they hurt. He dreamed of dark places. And watery figures. Faces laughing. And calling. Voices seemed to whisper secrets from inside his father's sea chest.

In the morning he stared at his itching fingers. And gasped. At first he couldn't take it in. He had ten fingernails. On each hand. Another row of nails had grown behind the first ones. Clean, pink, little fingernails.

He tore back the sheets and looked at his toes. The same thing had happened. A second row of toenails had burst out of the skin. They pointed forwards. Lapping slightly over the first row.

"Dad," he screamed. "Dad, Dad, Dad. Look. Something's wrong with me. My nails. I've got too many nai…" His voice trailed off. He remembered. Dad was down at the beach. On another secret search.

Lehman had been told never to go down the path to the cove. Dad had told him it was dangerous. And out of bounds.

But this was an emergency. Lehman stared in horror at his hands. He pulled at one of the new nails. It hurt when he tugged. It was real. It was there to stay. He staggered as he ran down the steep track to the beach. Tears of fright and anger streamed down his cheeks. His chest hurt. His breath tore harshly at his throat.

He pounded onto the hot sand and stared along the shore. His father was nowhere to be seen. Lehman took a guess and ran along the beach to his right. He came to a group of large rocks that blocked his way. The only way around was through the water. He waded into the gently lapping waves. The water came up to his armpits. He carefully strode on, feeling gently with his feet for rocky holes.

At the deepest point, the water came up to his chin. But he was nearly around the corner now. Lehman let his feet leave the bottom. He began to swim. He rounded the rocks and splashed into a small cove that he had never seen before.

9

His father was digging in the pebbles against a rocky wall. At first he didn't see Lehman. Then he looked up. And noticed the dripping figure staggering out of the waves. His face broke into a radiant smile. The look of someone who has found a pot of gold. Then he saw that it was Lehman and his face grew angry.

"I told you never to come here," he shouted. "I can't believe that you'd spy on me. You'll ruin everything. Go back. Go back." He wasn't just cross. He was furious.

Lehman said nothing. He just held out his hands. Turned the backs of his fingers towards his father. There was a long silence. His father's anger melted. He stared at the double row of nails. Silently Lehman pointed to his feet. They both gazed down.

"Oh, no," said Dad. "No. I never expected this. Not really."

"What is it?" yelled Lehman. "Am I going to die?"

"No. You're not going to die."

"I need a doctor," said Lehman.

"No," said Dad. "A doctor can't do anything. Not for that."

"What is it? What's wrong with me? You have to tell me."

They stared at each other. Both afraid.

Dad sat down on a rock. "I can't tell you. Not yet. What I'm looking for here. It's got something to do with it. If I find what I'm looking for it will be all right. You won't have to worry. But I can't tell. Not yet."

"What if you never find it?" said Lehman.

"I will," said Dad. "I have to."

Lehman scratched the back of his hands and up his arms. The itch was growing worse. And spreading.

Dad looked around as if he was frightened of Lehman seeing something. As though he had a guilty secret. "Go home," he said. "I'll pack my things and follow. We'll talk back at the house."

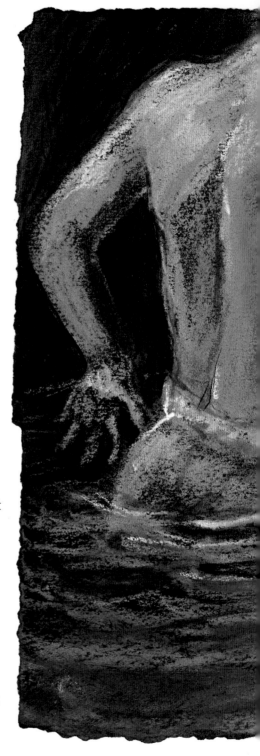

Lehman pushed into the water. His mind swirled. His arms itched. Something was terribly wrong. He turned around and shouted back. "What's going on? You're not telling. I've got a right to know."

Tears pricked his eyes. Tears of anger and frustration. Dad hung his head. "Go back," he called. "We'll talk. But not here."

Lehman swam out into the swell. He passed the furthest rock and headed back to the beach on the other side. Dad was out of sight now. Lehman's feet touched the bottom, and he walked through the water past a deep, black cave in the rocks.

Something moved inside.

The world froze. Lehman could hear the blood pumping in his head. A shiver spread over his skin like a wave. He choked off a cry. Two dark eyes stared out at him. He turned and thrashed through the water. Half swimming. Half running. Falling. Splashing in panic. He fell and sank under the surface. When he came up he snatched a frightened

glance back at the black space between the rocks. He caught a glimpse of a man's face. Staring. Watching. Hiding.

Lehman fled along the beach, stumbling in terror, not daring to look behind him. He didn't stop until he reached the bungalow. He rushed inside. The thin walls and open windows offered no protection. But he felt better. His breath slowed. His heart beat less loudly. He looked back down the track and wondered if Dad was safe.

He scratched his elbows. And then screamed. More nails had grown. Rows and rows of them. Along his fingers and the backs of his hands. And up over his wrists.

Perfectly formed fingernails lapped over each other. They looked like two gloves of armour.

The world around began to spin. Lehman felt dizzy. His legs wobbled. He looked down. The backs of his toes, feet, and ankles were covered too. A gleaming pair of toenail socks grew out of his skin. He opened his mouth to call out. And then fainted onto the floor.

When he awoke, the first thing Lehman saw was the photo of his mother. Her soft smile seemed to have faded. The pearl clip in her hair was dull. Then he realized that his eyes were half closed. He was staring at the world through his eyelashes. He suddenly remembered the nails. Was it a dream? He sat up and found himself on his bed. He stared at his hands. The nails had grown up his arms to his elbows. His legs were covered too. Toenails grew up to his knees.

Dad put out a hand and gently touched his shoulder. "It's okay," he said. "Everything is going to be all right. Don't worry."

Lehman smiled for a second. Dad was safe. Then he examined the nails. The smile disappeared. He was angry. "Don't worry," he yelled. "Don't worry. Look at my arms. And legs. I'm covered in nails. I'm not normal. What are we doing here? What are you looking for down on the beach?" He stared at the photo next to his bed. "What happened to my mother? I want to know what's going on."

The wind rattled the windows and shook the bungalow. A sultry storm was brewing up. Far down below, their boat tugged and pulled at the ropes that tied it to the pier.

Dad took a deep breath. "Okay," he said. "It's time I told you everything." He stood up and shut the shaking window. He raised his voice above the noise of the wind. "I don't know where to start," he said.

Lehman held up a nail-covered arm. "Start here," he cried. "What's happening to me?" As they looked, another row of nails slowly erupted from his left arm, just above the elbow. It was like watching a flower open in fast forward. Lehman felt nothing. It wasn't painful.

Dad stroked the nails gently. As if Lehman was a cat. "You're not sick," he said. "But I think more nails will grow."

"How many more nails? Will they grow on my face? On my head? On my chest?"

Dad gave a kindly smile. "Not your face. Maybe the rest of you though. I can't be sure. But I can find out. That's what I'm here for."

There was a long silence. "Are you looking for that man?" said Lehman.

"What man?" snapped Dad. His eyes were startled.

"I saw a face in the rocks. Down by the point. He was staring at me. Spying."

"What did he look like?" said Dad. His voice was shrill and urgent.

"I don't know. I was scared. I only saw his eyes. I ran off."

"This is it," yelped Dad. "This is what I've been waiting for. This is the answer to the problem." He hurried off to the window and looked down at the sea. The waves were crashing now. The wind whipped at them, tearing off their foamy tops and pelting them into the humid skies.

"I'm going," said Dad. "Wait here. Wait here. Everything will be all right."

"No way," said Lehman. "You're not leaving me behind again. I'm coming too."

Shutters banged and a blast of wind broke into the hut like a violent burglar. Everything shook.

"There's going to be a terrible storm," yelled Dad. "You can't come, it's too dangerous."

"If you go—I go," said Lehman. He looked his father straight in the eye. They stared at each other.

"This is a once-in-a-lifetime chance," said Dad. "He might go. I have to…"

"What's it got to do with this?" yelled Lehman. He held up his arms. The nails had crept up to his shoulders. And another row was growing. Budding like an ivory chain around his neck. "What about me? It's all right for you. Look at your skin. Normal. Look at me. Covered in nails. Don't you care?"

"It's because I care," said Dad. He had tears in his eyes. He tried to explain. "When we were here before. When you were young…"

"I don't remember," said Lehman. "You know I don't"

"No," said Dad. "But you were here. And your mother. And that man. He might. He's our only chance to…"

A terrible gust of wind shook the bungalow. Thunder rumbled in the distance. The sky was torn and savage. Dad stared outside. His face was as wild as the storm. "I have to go," he said. "Later. I'll explain later." He ran to the door and vanished into the lashing wind.

Lehman followed his father, still dressed in nothing but shorts. He didn't feel the raging wind. Or the stinging rain. He didn't notice the nails still growing and spreading. A worse fear had filled him. He was frightened for his father. Lehman couldn't see him but he knew that he was somewhere ahead. Down the track that led to the beach.

The wind screamed and howled. Tore at his hair. Stung his eyes. He hurried on and finally found his father. He was standing at the end of the track. Staring into the furious waves which dashed up the beach and crashed into the cliff. The rocks in which the stranger had hidden were nearly covered. They were cut off by the surf. There was no safe way to get to them.

Dad peered at the sand which was revealed as the sea sucked back each wave. He measured the distance to the rocks with his eyes. Then he turned and shouted over the noise of the wind. "Is that where he was? Is that where you saw the man?"

Lehman nodded and then grabbed his father's arm. "Don't go," he yelled. "It's too rough. You won't have a chance."

Dad snatched away his arm. He waited as a large wave began its sweep back from the beach. He jumped and ran along the sodden sand. His feet made deep, wet footprints which filled with water. The wave raced back into the sea, leaving the beach clear. A new wave ate the old and began its forward rush.

The desperate man was half-way. He sank up to his ankles with each step. The wet sand slowed him to a stumbling crawl. "Go," whispered Lehman. "Go, go, go." He watched the approaching wave grow. "Don't," he said. "Don't."

The wave took no notice. It raced hungrily up the beach. It swirled around Dad's ankles. Knocked him from his feet. Buried him in its angry foam.

Lehman squinted and peered into the water. His father was gone. The waves were empty. Then he saw a helpless bundle washing out into the deep. Dad raised an arm. And then another. He was swimming far out. His arms flayed. He seemed to be moving into deeper water. He was helpless against the strength of the sea. "I'm coming," yelled Lehman. He stepped forward, waiting for the next backwash.

But before he could move, he noticed Dad riding the crest of a wave. Surfing inwards at enormous speed. A tiny, helpless cork rushing forward towards the waiting cliff.

Lehman sighed with relief. And then fright. The wave was too big. It was going to run up to the cliff and kill itself on the rocks. It seemed to gather all its strength. It flung Dad full into the jagged boulders. And then left him, hanging helplessly on a small ledge.

Without another thought, Lehman jumped onto the sand. He had to get to Dad before the next wave began its run. He made it just in time. He grabbed the stunned man by his shirt and dragged him to his feet. Dad stumbled and leaned on Lehman as the next wave crashed around them.

It sucked and pulled at their legs. Tried to topple them. But Lehman felt a strange strength. It was almost as if the sea had no power over him. He dragged his father back to the steps where they sat sodden and panting. The disappointed waves swirled and smashed below them.

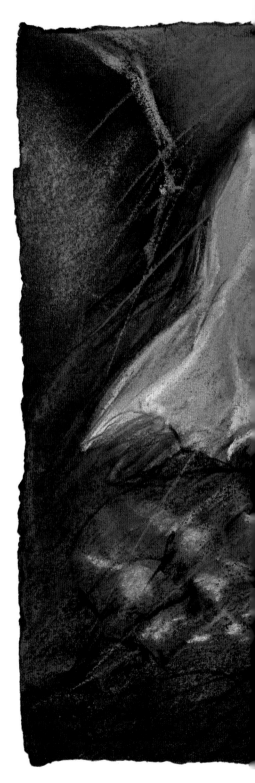

Dad tried to stand. He took a few steps like a drunken man. Lehman noticed a huge swelling on his father's head. A lump as big as a tennis ball. His eyes swiveled and he started to fall.

Lehman grabbed his father by the arm. He managed to drag him, stumbling up to the house. It took all his strength. His sides ached. His chest throbbed with pain. He burst through the door and dumped his father into the chair.

Dad stared out of the window. His eyes were glazed. As the wind dropped and the storm grew still, he held out a shaking arm. He pointed down to the beach. Then he drew a deep breath, shuddered, and was still.

Lehman knew that his father was dead. Silent tears trickled down his cheeks and splashed on the nails that covered his chest. He sat there like a sorrowful knight of old. A warrior in a coat of mail. Crying for a friend who had fallen.

All night Lehman sat. And all morning. He'd never seen a dead person before. He didn't know what to do. Finally he stood up and walked to the door. He looked out at the sea. He wanted help. But he didn't want anyone to come.

He knew he could never leave the island. Not while he was covered in nails. He couldn't go back to the world. A world that would laugh. Or stare and wonder. He could see himself sitting in a school desk. Raising an encrusted arm.

He walked back into the room and looked at Dad. He had to do it now. Or he never would. He gently closed his father's eyes. They were soft but cold. It was like shutting a book at the end of a story. A book which would never be opened again. But a book which would never be forgotten. Not for as long as the waves beat on the lonely beach below.

Dad would be heavy. Lehman knew that. He had to dig a grave close to the house.

He chose a sandy spot that overlooked the sea. Lehman could just see the rocks jutting out where he had seen the face. He started to talk to his father as if he was still there. Standing by him.

"This is the place," he said. "You can see down there. Maybe what you wanted will come. Whatever it was."

The sand was soft. He dug easily and soon had a shallow trench hollowed in the sand. It came up to his knees. He didn't want to make it too deep. Not because the work was hard. But because he couldn't bear to drop his father into a gaping hole. Something might bump. Or break.

Lehman returned to the silent man. He grabbed his father under the arms and tugged him slowly out of the door. The dead weight was heavy. Dad's feet dragged and bumped down the steps.

Lehman lowered him gently into the grave.

He looked down at the silent figure, stretched out. It was as if he was sleeping peacefully in the sand. Lehman picked up the shovel. But something was wrong. He felt bad. As if he had to do something that would hurt. Then he knew what it was. He couldn't put a shovelful of sand on his father's face. Even though he was dead.

He fetched an old newspaper from inside. Then he looked at the gentle face for the last time and covered it with the paper. He filled the hole with sand and smoothed it down. He had no strength left to make a gravestone so he pushed the shovel into the sand. And left it standing as a tall marker.

"Goodbye, Dad," he said.

Lehman stood and stared out to sea. The sun glinted on the thousands of nails that covered almost every part of him. He looked like a tall lizard man. Standing. Waiting. Daring an invader to come.

There was no boat on the water. He didn't care. He didn't want anyone to see him as he was, covered in nails. A great feeling of loneliness filled him. As far as he knew, there was no one else in the world like him.

He walked inside and looked in the mirror. His face was clear. But his chest, back, arms, and legs were covered with the new nails. He suddenly opened a drawer. And pulled out some nail clippers. He wondered if he would have to spend his life clipping thousands of nails as they grew. He laughed wildly and threw the clippers out of the open window.

It had taken him all afternoon to dig the grave.

The sun was beginning to sink lower in the sky. In an hour or two it would be dark. And he was alone. He wondered if he should lock the windows. And bolt the door. He knew that tonight—when the dark came—he would be frightened.

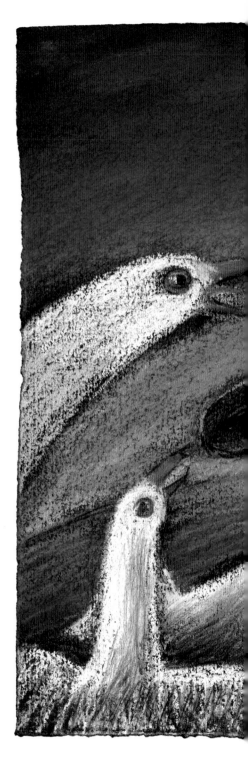

The face in the cave would come. Creeping. Stealing up the path. Wandering in the shadows. He knew that he would jump at every sound. He would try not to sleep. But in the end sleep would come. And so would the unknown man.

He jumped to his feet. "You won't get me," he shouted. "I'll get you."

He ran outside and sharpened a long stick with the axe. Now he had a spear. He marched down the path towards the beach. His legs felt weak. His stomach was cold and heavy. He wanted to turn. And run. And hide.

But he forced himself on until he reached the beach. The sea was still and blue. It lapped gently on the sandy beach. The wild waves had gone. Lehman strode along the sand toward the rocks. And the cave.

He shuddered even though the air was warm. He gripped the spear tightly with his nailed fingers. The tide was out, and the small cave now opened onto the sand. He reached the entrance and peered into the gloom.

There were soft, dripping noises. And the sound of steady breathing. Someone was in there.

"Come out," he shrieked. His voice cracked and ended in a squeak. He coughed and tried again. "Come out, whoever you are." The words echoed in the cave. Then something moved. He thought he heard a slippery, rustling noise.

His courage fled. He started walking backwards, too frightened to turn around.

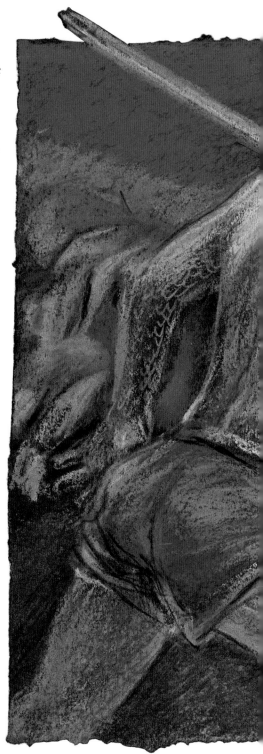

Three people came out of the cave. If people is the word. Two men. And a smaller one. They wore no clothes. But instead, were covered from neck to toe—in nails.

Lehman felt faint. He couldn't take it in. He wondered if this island gave people the terrible nail disease.

They smiled at him. Warm, friendly smiles. The child giggled nervously. The nail people were wet. They had been in the sea. Water glistened and sparkled from their nails. They shone like neat rows of wet glass.

One of the men pointed into the deep water further our. A swift shadow like a shark circling moved far down. It rushed toward the shore with the speed of a train. Then burst out of the water and back in again.

Lehman caught a glimpse of a sparkling fish tail. And fair hair. It swirled several times. And then climbed onto a rock. A woman with long golden hair. And a fish tail covered in nails.

The men laughed. Their chuckles sounded like bubbles bursting out of the water. Lehman stared at the nails, which shivered as they moved. He spoke aloud. Half to himself. Half to them. "Not nails," he said, "but scales."

He turned back to the mermaid. In her hair, she wore a golden clip, set with pearls. The same pin that he had seen every day in his mother's photograph.

In that moment Lehman knew that while his father had been a man, his mother was a mermaid.

She beckoned to him, calling him out into the water. Then she dived down under the rippling surface. The mermen nodded at him, pointing out to sea. Like Lehman, they had legs rather than a tail.

Lehman walked. And walked. And walked. The waves closed over his head. He opened his mouth and took a deep breath of water. It passed through his new gills with a fizz of bubbles. His head was filled with lightness. And happiness. He began to swim, deep down, following his mother.

Then, for a second, he remembered something. He burst upwards faster and faster and plunged out of the water like a dolphin. He snatched one last look at the island. And saw, high on a hill, a small mound. A shovel stood pointing to the bright sky above. He knew now why his father had brought him here. A fish-boy could only be happy in one place—the ocean.

Lehman waved goodbye and then plunged down far below the surface. And followed his family out to sea.